Diggers
and Trucks

by Frances Ridley

BRENT LIBRARIES	
04336813	
PETERS	12-Mar-2009
£3.99	BRWIL

Contents

Words in **bold** are explained in the glossary.

Copyright © **ticktock Entertainment Ltd 2008**
First published in Great Britain in 2008 by **ticktock Media Ltd.**,
Unit 2, Orchard Business Centre, North Farm Road,
Tunbridge Wells, Kent, TN2 3XF

We would like to thank: Penny Worms, Alix Wood and the National Literacy Trust.

ISBN 978 1 84696 766 5

Printed in China

A CIP catalogue record for this book is available from the British Library.
All rights reserved. No part of this publication may be reproduced, copied, stored in a retrieval
system or transmitted in any form or by any means electronic, mechanical, photocopying, recording
or otherwise without prior written permission of the copyright owner.

Picture credits: b=bottom; c=centre; t=top; r=right; l=left
Alvey & Towers: 4-5c, 6-7c, b/c: cr; Caterpillar: 16-17c; Contruction Photo Library: 16cl; Corbis: 3b, 8-
9c; JCB: 2t, 20-21, 21t, b/c: cl; John Deere: 22/23c, 23tr; Komatsu: 10-11c, 11t, 14-15c, 15t; Letourneau
Inc: 12-13c, 13t; Mack Trucks: 8cl; Oshkosh: 18-19c, 19t; Peterbilt: 4cl;

Every effort has been made to trace the copyright holders, and we apologise in advance for any
unintentional omissions. We would be pleased to insert the appropriate acknowledgements
in any subsequent edition of this publication.

Peterbilt 379 Road Truck

The Peterbilt 379 is an **articulated** road truck. It is made up of two parts: a **tractor unit** and a trailer.

Tractor unit

The Peterbilt carries heavy loads. It needs a big engine!

Mercedes-Benz Actros

The Actros is a cabover truck.
The driver's cab is over the engine.
The cabs are **soundproofed** to
keep out engine noise.

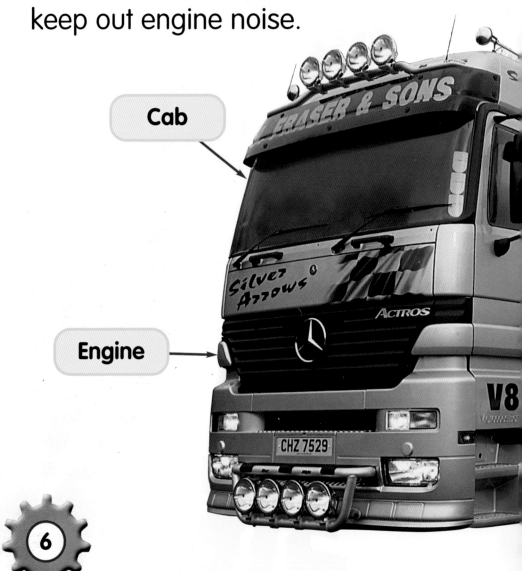

Cab

Engine

Actros cabs are very comfortable for long journeys.

Mack Road Train

Road trains are trucks that pull three or more trailers. All Mack trucks have a silver bulldog on the front.

The biggest Mack truck
is 53 metres long and
has four fuel tanks!

Haulpak 930E Dump Truck

The Haulpak 930E dump truck is huge. The driver climbs a ladder to get into the cab!

The Haulpak works in **quarries** and mines.

It carries rock and earth
in its bucket.

Bucket

930E

LeTourneau L-2350 Wheel Loader

The LeTourneau L-2350 Wheel Loader digs up earth and rocks. Then it dumps them into a truck.

The driver uses a joystick to make the bucket dig and dump.

Can you see how big it is?

Komatsu D575A Super Dozer

Bulldozers break up earth and push it around.

The Super Dozer is bigger than any other bulldozer!

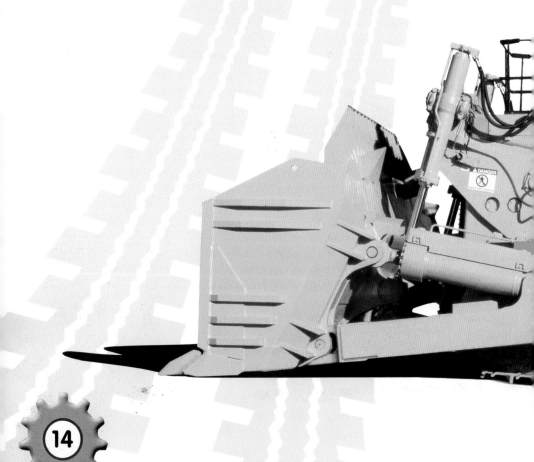

It has tracks to ride over muddy or bumpy ground.

Tracks

Cat 385L Excavator

The Cat 385L Excavator is a huge digging machine. It weighs 83.5 tonnes.

Its long arm has a bucket to scoop up soil.

16

The cab can turn all the way round.

Oshkosh S-Series Mixer Truck

The Oshkosh Mixer Truck mixes sand, gravel and cement in its drum. The drum turns round slowly to make concrete.

Chute

18

At the building site, the concrete comes down a chute.

Drum

JCB Backhoe Loader

The JCB Backhoe Loader has a bucket and an arm with a shovel. The arm picks up earth and moves it away.

Bucket

JCB has a stunt team of Dancing Diggers!

Arm

John Deere 9750 Combine

The John Deere 9750 Combine cuts down wheat. It strips the grain from the stalks. It stores the grain in a tank and leaves the stalks behind.

Grain

This is the John Deere badge.

Glossary

articulated A truck in two parts.

quarries Places where rocks and stones are dug out of the earth.

shovel A scoop used to lift and throw rocks and earth.

soundproofed A way of making noise quieter.

tractor unit The tractor's cab, engine and front wheels.

Index

24